One Guy's Military Journey:

Poetic Reflections

Chris "FOG" Barnes

Printed by IngramSpark.

First Printing, 2020.

www.facebook.com/One-Guys-Military-Journey-109216174095395/

Contents

Section 1 – History...............................1

The Soldier's Boots
Our Return
American Generations I
American Generations II
Ditches

Section 2 – Service..............................13

The Letter Home
Luck Charms
The Day I Didn't Die
The Time Between I
The Time Between II
Changing of the Guard
I Volunteered For This

Section 3 – Senses..............................33

The Smell
Silence & Silence (Reimagined)
The Din
The Eyes
The Weight

Section 4 – Aftermath................................47

The First Week of December
Avoidance
The Recurring Nightmare
The Night I Should've Quit Drinking
Scars & Scars (Reimagined)
The Stigma
The Screams I Hear

More Thoughts....................................67

The Bottom of a Bottle
Time I
Time II
My Plea
Our Why
To The 22

Dedicated to those who serve,
those who served, and those who
want to know more

Thanks to folks who helped
review different verses including
Omar, Travis, Charity, Cathy,
Dad, and particularly, my wife

And a special thanks to Travis
Yewell Photography for the
cover artwork

I have spent over 12 years with various symptoms of moderate Post-Traumatic Stress Disorder (PTSD) after several combat tours. One of these tours included a role to quickly and efficiently perform crime scene investigation outside the wire, meaning off the base, for activities containing explosives and explosive devices, before or after the explosion occurred. Being in a combat zone comes with the inherent risk of witnessing horrible events, but with the position and job I had while deployed, horrific events became regular occurrence, which is where a majority of my combat-related stress comes from. I certainly never thought joining the Air Force in my particular responsibility that I would be placed in the situations that have caused this internal conflict, but in war, everyone has their role to play.

I started writing after almost 9 years of trying to handle my symptoms on my own, as a way to redistribute all the issues and topics that had been bottled up for all those years. Although often difficult to rehash these images and scenes, sometimes causing the PTSD symptoms to escalate with added anger or new nightmares, by writing I was able to slowly shed some of these burdens onto the paper and off of my shoulders. I don't personally believe PTSD can be completely healed, but I do believe that cognitive therapy in the verbal and written form can help reduce or alleviate some of the symptoms.

Beyond my own therapy, and after having put my honest stories and heart into these verses, I discovered further purposes for producing this book. If I can help other veterans and sufferers of PTSD through these verses, my primary goal for this book is achieved. Even more so, if I can provide you with the words that clarify what you are feeling or experiencing to your loved ones and friends, then I will have accomplished my second goal with this book. I have used these poems myself to speak transparency and express clarity about my experiences to members of my own family, and I believe it can do the same for you. I hope you enjoy these poems, but even more so, I hope they help.

These stories and ideas are a mixture of poetry and prose writing, as I utilized different formats to express the feelings of each poem. Over time, some of the original writings were altered within the same context to create a different form of poetry (i.e. a prose poem or free verse into a rhymed poem or lyric), and I included a few of those poems as well. As a warning, these poems speak directly to instances of war and the effects of combat PTSD, and could also be inferred to other forms of PTSD. Please understand that the writing is meant to be intense, to heighten strong sentiment, and may cause high levels of emotion and recollections for a wide variety of people.

<u>Section 1 – History</u>

I began to enjoy history in high school, and became more captivated by military history in particular after I joined. Some of the stories of war heroes and military leaders I read as a teenager aided in my final decision to enter the ranks. History provides us not only with a glimpse into the past, but sets a marker for precedent and often acts as a guide for what to do and not to do in the profession of arms. Many of these poems started out as general topics I wanted to write about, and ended up turning into multi-day research projects to find the right historical names, backgrounds, and information to make them stand out. You will also find a mix of writing styles in this section, some of them my own design.

My pick – "The Soldier's Boots." I really enjoyed the research I performed for this poem, and hope that comes through with the names, places, and types of boots worn during the recent history of warfare. These verses started with the notion that it is difficult to understand what someone is going through until you have walked a mile in their shoes. This same notion applies to having worn boots in connection to the service of your country, and the verses flowed from there.

The Soldier's Boots

We pull them on daily with weighted sentiment, one at a time; first over the toes, sliding past the arches, and finally tugging up and over the heel. We tightly knot the laces, tucking in the excess strings, fasten buckles, shine the scuffs off the toe cap, secure the straps; we worry over imperfections, as our footwear is a visible requisite of our meticulous dress. We firmly marry leather to ankle and blouse the bottom hem of each pant leg over the upper lip as our final preparatory measure to complete the ensemble and move forward with the duty ahead; the soldier's boots.

They march headlong, rhythmically beating the ground with Russet's measured tread, a procession in military manner that can parade for a dignitary or forge into battle. These same boots advanced through Europe to Pershing's waiting trenches, headway into the icy mire fought seven feet deep and strident through a dash across no man's land; the soldier's boots.

They hike onward, steadily crossing the remote wilderness, through the dense woods of Boondocker's treacherous trails, taking their constitutional excursion to meet the enemy's front line. These boots traversed the skies and explored high and low country to stand at Eisenhower's forested front, fighting the bulging enemy through copse and thicket, trekking eastward; the soldier's boots.

They trudge ahead, gradually shuffling through impenetrable jungle and murky bush, a laborious slog in Saran-

2

wrapped feet down Ho Chi Minh's path. These same boots
wearily exerted athwart Westmoreland's tangled tropics,
exhaustively sloughed the wilds covered in pointed traps and
lethal snares; the soldier's boots.

They walk forward, increasingly springing step by
tempered step across desert dunes in impermeable heat, running
headlong to the filthy streets of Fallujah and Kabul. These
brandless boots swiftly trotted over the sandbanks of
Schwarzkopf's left hook, rapidly combatting the stings of
incoming fire and intense sandstorms; the soldier's boots.

Whether black or brown leather, spit or Kiwi polish, or
rough side out with a mission application, a soldier's boots
communicate stories and tales across generations of combat
warriors. Boots on the ground, our physical presence on a
battlefield; a new boot in the unit, our malign slang for new
recruits; a pair of boots at a standing memorial or placed below
the battlefield cross, a stark reminder of the ultimate sacrifice.

Sole to sole, shoe to boot, there no way to understand the
weight of these boots, the burden of what they have seen
navigating the many pathways of war. No one else knows how our
feet might feel if they've never spent time in the soldier's boots.

Our Return

Our tour is over; but not everyone gets to come home; others
continue to march open column dispersed through unforgiving
terrain,
continue to convoy down hostile roads,
continue to survive captive in the enemy's prison,
continue to breathe the foreign oxygen full of dust and sand, or
jungle moisture and humidity, or the icy air freezing your insides as
it hits your lungs.

With mixed emotions, worrying for those still in the fray yet frantic
and grateful for a taste of home, we ascend the gangway to the ship
with heavy hearts, we board the ramp of the behemoth aircraft
with anticipation, that it will take us safely across the wide, blue
expanse back to the shores of our origin.

Our arrival, the pivotal entrance to the homeland we fought for, is
met with a myriad of reactions. Some are greeted with pomp and
circumstance, official celebrations for their triumphant conquest,
grand ceremonies of victory and pride, parades provided by a
cheering society, family and loved ones welcoming them home
with open arms.

Others are hailed with vile contempt, formal protests for their
warmongering invasion, striking resistance of arrogance and defeat,
processions of a confrontational public who spurn them with open
hostility, disrespectful insults, and spit in their faces.

An unfortunate few are received with nothing but a lonesome walk
to the bus station, significant others or family long gone or moved
on having been deprived of their presence, broken relationships

and shattered homes, an emptier and hollow world, alone without their brothers fighting by their side.

Our return, our swan song of jubilant survival against odds often stacked against us, can quickly convert from a familial, personal festivity to a forlorn period of emptiness and desensitization. We miss the camaraderie of battle, desire for the safety of our brothers and sisters, and hunt newspapers and correspondence daily for information and names of those lost since we departed. Our bodies and minds primed for conflict every second, every day create acrimonious voids in the mundane routines of daily life.

We continue to think as though we are still fighting,
continue to keep watchful eyes on exits and strangers,
continue to stare into the distance while lost in thought,
continue to startle at innocuous booming sounds,
continue to crave the high that comes from primal battle.

For in our return, our physical battle is over; but the war is far from won.

American society screams the generational gap, a chasm that separates old from young, a canyon of rage divorcing blue collars from university pupils.

> *What have you to offer us but a dying world, outdated ideas, and old-fashioned rules?*

> *These young people have a craving for handouts, no deference to authority, and lack the drive to survive in this world.*

Year after year, decade after decade, the discourse continues with fuming dialogue of culpability and denunciation for who is truly at fault.

> *You have stolen from us that which is priceless — our future!*

> *We prepared an ideal platter, overflowing with that which we desired when we were young.*

And yet, when young become old and old become dust, these rifts remain open, these splits stay fragmented as the next generation blames their circumstances on the ones who suffered for their modern conveniences.

Generation after generation, the American vision endeavors past fissure and cleft headlong through the ages, onward from the steam engine to the rise of digital technologies, forward from industry to information. The single commonality that binds us together is the ransom of our kin, hastily delivered in the early juncture from boy to man or girl to woman, to the forlorn wastelands of our father's wars.

The Lost, the Greatest, the Silent, the Boomers, Gen X, Millennials, all generations former and forthcoming; society contributes sons and daughters, mothers and fathers, aunts and uncles to the one percent and country to fight for freedom, battle against brutality, skirmish for sovereignty, to clash in combat against cruelty and callousness with little regard for social order splits that swallow civilian citizens in their sans-swaying standpoints.

> *I choose to fight now, so my sons and daughters do not have to fight* (repeat for generations).

> *War does not care if you are Jew or Gentile, Christian or Muslim or Atheist, Mid-Western or Pacific Islander, East Coast or West Coast, Republican or Democrat or Independent, 18 or 36 or 62, white or brown or black, farmer or manager or producer, married or single; there is no discrimination, there is no determination made by war.*

And for some, we fortunate few, we devil dogs and zoomies, we ground pounders and squids and coasties, we one percenters across American generations, we silently trudge over crack and gap with each decade that passes with only cursory glances to the rifts and chasms of our peers' perspectives.

For their sacrifice, they suffer; from grandfather to father to son,
from grandmother to mother to daughter, they agonize; the trauma
of war creates excessive stress too copious for some to bear, a
disorder marching through the decades with no concern for
generational titles.

We pass down not peace and treaty, nor harmony and agreement;
instead we offer stories that haunt our dreams, accounts of
troubled distress, loss of friends and humanity to the next
generation who fights in our stead, who must shoulder a cratered
society's burden like a heavy coat and soundlessly trudge and
march into the next passing decade. And each generation's
inheritance is the weighty promise that we remain steadfast, ready
to fight when called.

Ditches

If I wanted to sketch a small portrait for you
Of what we remember of the things we went through
As they clash in our minds with the world as we know it,
The *ditches* may truly describe it and show it.

Now *ditches* as people most commonly see
Are channeling water, perhaps to some trees
Or to crops that need extra water to grow,
Or to drain it away or maintain its flow.

But there, the *ditches* are pestilence full,
A pandemic of odors, at your nostrils they pull.
The plague of old fruit as it rots in the sun,
An outbreak of aromas, my senses undone.
A contagion of sewage, and garbage, and clothes,
The smell of their virus, their afflictions and woes.
Strewn litter and germs from a roving cyclone,
Reeking of animal corpses and bones,
Their blood and their guts so callously thrown
Down disease-ridden paths for which they were known.
The memory of those *ditches* won't leave me alone.

Compare and contrast this to the *ditches* we used
During our childhoods to keep us amused.
Because here, the *ditches* are possibilities full,
Let's talk about how, through some memories we pull.
Some driveways are built over top of the *ditch*,
Making solid steep angles, and filling a niche,
As a ramp used to launch our old bikes way up high,
Giving us the sensation of a kite in the sky.

Some *ditches* would fill with the passing of rain,
Flooding inches of water unable to drain.
We swam and we played with ardor and fain,
Until mothers came out to shout and constrain.
The memory of those *ditches* when life was humane.

At times we used *ditches* as bounds for a field,
Or a natural buffer as a snowball fight shield.
And there, kids could use these *ditches* the same,
As a boundary to set when playing their game.
But if the ball dared travel down into that trench,
Would you risk losing your shoes to the stench?
The slop would be sticky, like wet cement or glue,
It would fasten to footwear, and gone was your shoe.
For forces in country, these same bounds were created
As *ditches* were used to keep convoys abated,
To delay or to trap our trucks in their place
Oil ignited in *ditches* to keep us encased,
So the flames would reach out, lick at our face,
And all we would want is to get back to the base.
Then the enemy attacks, playing their ace,
Only some of us survived through God-given grace,
The memory of those *ditches*, what we seek to erase.

We don't always use *ditches* in ways they intended,
Both places have rules that are simply amended.
At home, cars would park in our *ditches* to show
Where the party was at or where our friends go.
Parking at angles on grass or concrete,
Ditches were used instead of the street.
You don't dare park your truck in a *ditch* over there,
You stuck to the streets, making sure they were bare.

The threat was the trash, always laden with traps,
With bombs so giant they make bridges collapse.
Or the bodies we found in the muck and the mire,
Some were just children they forced to expire,
And leading away from them, a green and red wire,
The bodies all stuffed with explosive attire,
The air all around swiftly full of hellfire,
The memory of those *ditches* makes me want to retire.

And now you understand this equivalency
And the fact that our *ditches* have disparity
As they clash in our minds from the world we have seen,
Their definitions have changed from the time in between.

Section 2 – Service

As a part of cognitive processing therapy, one of several types of PTSD therapy that I have been through over the past few years, they ask you to write about your experiences during service and some of the harsh realities of combat. Most of these poem topics resurfaced from those therapy sessions and into the verses that follow. This group of poems consist of occurrences and difficulties that I observed during my military years, primarily related to combat deployments, and a few personal accounts of my time in service.

My Pick – "The Letter Home." One of the most difficult things I have ever had to do was write a letter to my family, which was to be provided to them upon my death by a friend of close confidant from combat. I still have the letter I wrote from my first combat deployment saved in a personal file, and I was able to use that for inspiration for the words and phrases in this piece. I still have a tough time reading the final lines, imagining my family having to read them in their grief.

<u>The Letter Home</u>

Four months; 121 days; nearly 175,000 minutes into a year-long deployment. Gunfire aimed in my direction, dozens of firefights, hundreds of explosions, seeing the deadliest of weapons used against warrior and civilian alike, and finally a brother's battlefield cross forced me to park in front of a computer and write it; the letter you reluctantly but reliably hand to a brother for delivery; the "if I die" letter…the letter home.

I lacked belief in Death; if the letter failed to exist, it's not my time. I lacked gumption; the toughest words to put on paper. I lacked desire; no aspirations to say farewell to my family. I lacked understanding; who accepts the message or do I write several letters for family. I lacked empathy; what verses would help their understanding and mourning…the letter home.

The handheld dispatch delivery, an important distinction for the brother who must carry the burden in their pocket. The appeal for in-person visitation to transport the document for the harshest face-to-face; only the closest of brothers. To request that your death to be tougher on them, for your demise to add to their shouldered load…the letter home.

The first paragraph; what to say. The foundation to such a significant manuscript, and yet I blather about something happening. For something to be in place as a just in case. Redeemed from this opening drivel, I state I knew the consequences of my volunteerism; my life was filled by my choices; no blame is to be placed…the letter home.

The next passage; what to say. No more prattling, talk about them. My family; our lives becoming closer over time, the proximity of family to make visits more abundant, drinking in the enjoyment of their company on journey's home. Now the hard part; I wish I could see your children grow into great men and women; I am watching over you all…the letter home.

The third section; what to say. Less jabber, get to the point. I am honored to fight, yet pride is overshadowed by your painful loss; I depart for a dwelling with no war, yet grim to envision not going home; content to have served brother, country, and God with the ultimate sacrifice. Knowing better, yet I still pray for swift mourning; your families will need you, move forward with enjoyable memories…the letter home.

The last part; what to say, the final words my family will hear and see. More babble of how hard it is to write, how I sought to come home but God's intentions were met, or repeating the just in case prattling; I evaded finishing. I think of you every day, knowing you pray for and think of me daily; I dodged the conclusion. You have made this deployment easier with letters and calls home; stop avoiding it.

I will miss you until we are together again in a better place. I love you with all my heart. Remember, I am with those who have gone before, waiting patiently for that day when we will see each other again and watching over you forever. I love you. Bud.

The letter home.

Bestowing good luck; or perhaps superstition held as irrational belief that inanimate objects can alter one's future. History displays thousands of trinkets assuming powers for their bearer; the four leaf clover, horseshoe, acorn, scarab beetle, rabbit's foot on a chain, a ladybug landing on your outstretched hand, even a beloved team's jersey or cap worn to bring a win on game day. Control over the coming time or simple delusional fallacy, imparting invisible fortune to those who bear them and believe.

The soldier is no different, craving luck from objects while heading to battle. Romans marched with images and amulets of the winged phallus, the believed source of their power. European soldiers alleged the pig held similar influence, as metal boar emblems were their talisman. Today, we endure tradition, pilfering these customary objects as our own safety net, carried continuously to escape injury or death on the battlefield. Beyond clovers and animal feet, we pack personalized lighters, even those who do not smoke; coins, lucky when discovered heads up; a picture of family, significant other, or children affixed to our helmets; an ace, particularly the Ace of Spades; even soldier skeptical in superstition not chancing a forgotten object consistently carried into combat.

But there remains objects we do not speak of, never overlooked or left behind; those meant for when luck runs out. For generations gone, the objects unnecessary as soldiers fought until the battle was done or their death dealt. Avoiding dishonor, daggers or swords meant for swift movement of personal sacrifice in the face of shameful capture. Small bottles of poison, cyanide pills adorned the neck, held within the mouth, awaiting the last possible second before seizure. The single bullet, awaiting the extinguishment of ammo and an imminent overrun position.

We carry these burdensome items with purpose; a family and brothers never observing video of a radical enemy cutting my head from my body. We carry these objects with worried reluctance; the cold anxiety of running down to my final bullet. We carry this luck in enduring hope; to survive and go home to those who wait.

<u>The Day I Didn't Die</u>

Today was the day I didn't die.

It began like any other day,
I heard the phone ring from bed where I lay.
I knew it was my turn to leave for the fray,
So I sat up quickly, and got on my way.

I prayed, today is the day I don't die.

The call was relayed, the team found a bomb,
We asked for position and relay of comm.
As always, the mission we received with aplomb,
To again fight against the power of Saddam.

I repeated, today is the day I don't die.

In a much hurried state I was ready,
No longer waking up and unsteady,
I grabbed my boxed meal, spaghetti;
I favored this more than the veggie.

We met with security to convey
And talk through the concern of the day.
A swift chat with the chaplain to pray,
Then out the gate, quickly on our way.

I implored to God, today is the day I don't die.

The ride to the scene took an hour,
Through streets and ditches smelling sour.

Traffic was thick despite the power
Of the truck's gunner bidding them to cower.

I thought, today is the day I don't die.

Finally we arrived to the scene,
We found it secure, and safe, and clean.
An ordinary day it did seem,
Another bomb could be visibly seen.

First action was to run to the trunk,
Get the robot to raise from its bunk.
It would spy from amid all the junk
On the roadside, this I-E-D punk.

Once more, I prayed today is the day I don't die.

I was out of the truck at the squeak,
Of the comm. in my ear as they speak,
To call me forward to give my critique,
And perform my forensic technique.

Then the bomb went off with a crack,
And ping off the truck went the flak.
No way could we thwart the attack,
As proper intel and data we lack.

I said, today is the day I didn't die.

As falling robot remains decreases,
Chief and I move to collect all the pieces.
The safe distance extends and increases,
I turn, and my deed swiftly ceases.

Shit...today is the day I die.

Before I could say to him stop,
A hidden car with smoke from the top.
Not a boom or a bang, but a pop,
In that instant, I felt my heart drop.

Today is the day I die.

Shocked, we looked and we said,
Counting legs, and arms, and head,
We're lucky to be alive and not dead,
No blood on this day was shed.

Today was the day I didn't die.

As we looked further into that car,
A door was found slightly ajar.
A dozen mines were seen from afar,
But the bomb's wiring, completely sub-par.

Dumb luck on that day, I agree.
I survived a V-B-I-E-D.
Not the last, I survived total three.
And there, to live is no guarantee.

Today was a day I didn't die.

The Time Between I

I was handed a rather large decision to make,
Of where and how long to take my short break.
It could affect family and friends who I'd missed,
Positives, negatives, I created my list.

Go home to see family and friends for two weeks,
With parties, embraces, what's there to critique?
Could I go back to see them, the same as before?
Would they be happy with time, or left wanting more?
Would I crack and crumble, if they asked me those questions
Of battle or killing, could I show an expression?
Of course they would want me to tell them some stories,
But how to convey that it's not about glory?
Its sisters you've watched catch lead in their chest,
Or brothers you've seen with no legs and the stress,
Or of how all your thoughts leave your head in a mess,
To go home with this burden, how can I say yes?

Or do I travel around to see other places,
And potentially fall out of my family's good graces?
I could climb mountains on up to the peak,
Or relax on the beach in the sand for a week.
I could visit the structures of a city well-known,
And see how its history has been overgrown.
Could I make it a year without seeing my people,
As I still had another six months' worth of sequel?
The people I meet, could they see what I am,
A soldier at war but sent out on the lam?
Would my friends and my family see me for my sham?
Could I rest under waves of the stress that slam
Against those high built walls, crumbling my dam?

22

Damned if you don't, and damned if you do,
My body is tight with each twist of the screw,
My brain is pounding, my mood has gone blue,
I can't hold it together, not even with glue,
My thoughts have collapsed, I sit and I stew,
To go home or not? To see something new?
Around and around, I couldn't push through,
But then, I had it and did it; I finally knew.

I toss and I turn with the decision I've made,
But I knew in the end it was my family I craved.
I've had enough of fresh places for now,
The last six months of surviving somehow.
The decision was made to travel on home,
Back to the place where I'd become grown.
Brothers departed to visit places unknown,
And others, like me, towards home the winds blown.
Any doubts I push off with a hard mental shove,
I'm off on a plane colored white as a dove,
To the friends that I greet with a five high above,
To the warm embraces of the family I love,
To collapse in the arms that fit like a glove,
To relax in the peace of the stress I'm free of.

The Time Between II

It didn't quite hit me, this decision I made,
When the plane landed, the stress would invade.
I didn't run through the airport to those waiting hugs.
I inched my way past those shops like a slug.
I stopped in the restroom I think twice on my way.
It was all I could do, I crept and belayed.
Why did I do this? I don't really know,
I wanted to see them, and yet I went slow.
Maybe my mind said I didn't deserve
Such an arrival, but I built up my nerve,
And went down to luggage, then thrown for a curve,
To see my dad crying, second time to observe,
Yet I lacked the emotion to feel even concern.

I cannot be sure when I began to feel cold,
Almost zero emotion, despite my parent's tight hold.
We peel away from the hug to get on with the plan,
Collecting the luggage, we went out to the van.
They caught me up on all the comings and goings
Of family and friends, now known from unknowing.
I learned of a death in our family in winter,
But still my emotional wall did not splinter.
We pulled up to the house, my sisters' form rare,
Their joy and their tears set ablaze with a flare
At the sight of their brother, a God-answered prayer,
Returning from war where he gave them a scare
That he may not return from way over there.
I felt little emotion; why didn't I care?

The week was planned out with parties and cookouts,
Traveling the towns and driving the old routes.
The family was ecstatic I had come into town,
But the world all around me was beginning to drown.
While driving the roads, I'd see trash and freak out,
Slamming the brakes, jerk the wheel with a shout.
In the middle of having a chat with a friend,
My thousand yard stare I'd have to defend.
My anger, frustration, it was starting show,
Breaking that barrier I'd wanted only to grow.

See it wasn't all sunshine and rainbows for me.
While they reveled on with such elation and glee,
I headed outside to be all alone,
I'd sit in a chair in the garage on my own,
Not trying to ruin the party they'd thrown,
But there I would be, staring out in a zone.
My dad would come out and sit down with a groan,
He was quiet but near, his jaw clenched to the bone,
The lone vet around who simply had known
Why I needed my space, my face barely shown.

And then it was time for me to head back,
Again my emotions showed nary a crack.
My family was torn that I had to return,
Saying "stay safe" in their voice of concern.
And once again tears and sorrow had formed,
Like gnats all around, family started to swarm,
All hugs and caresses, I needed to leave.
They acted as though they needed to grieve.
Then off to the airport, my parents were last
To transfer the love that they wanted to pass.
I turned in my luggage and was handed my ticket
To get past security, crowds dense as a thicket.

I arrived on the plane, and started to think,
While the steward ran off to get me my drink,
That relaxing from stress while at home was a joke,
That I should've just went to the beach for a stroke,
That civilian understanding was far less awoke,
They could never wrench off us this burden and yolk.
That good-byes only happen through tears and a choke,
As my mind only saw the bombs and the smoke;
Because our mind never rests, a race going for broke,
That soldiers can't rest at home with their folk.

<u>Changing of the Guard</u>

Time is expiring, this lengthy stretch of days into weeks and months of deployed stress, this extended stay in hostile tension, this prolonged absence from family and friends is finally nearing completion. Before departure, one obligation, a single duty, a solitary responsibility remains; the changing of the guard. No matter their numerical age or quantity of military years, these newbies are treated as fledgling colts, mere babes in this aggressive undertaking. Throughout history, we label them rookie, draftee, replacement, FNG, greenie, but the designations matter naught as they must step over our unknown line from combat liability to proven respectability, from green to battle-ready so our exit may be deemed possible.

No method exists to pass the reins of an unbridled stagecoach, to teach these green newcomers the sum of all knowledge we gained about a consistently fluctuating enemy. We can hold their hand as they tighten a bolt, show them process and checklist steps, provide changeover briefings describing the enemy to a penultimate degree, draw them maps of chokepoints and regular ruses of explosive devices and snipers; but these cannot compare to living a day in the life.

Our prolonged presence in country concludes with a phase rampant with trying strain and crippling anxiety, as their first day or week outside the wire is our last; a perilous time before the sendoff elation, a closing curtain where hope and luck are our saving graces. My first changing of the guard struck with two ragged devices shredding tires and chipping armor, providing seismic shakings as my final farewell; my second, a sniper's bullet fragmenting the wall just inches from my face, a suitable send-off from my last combat mission. A terrible death to experience in combat are those with orders prepped for departure, with a ticket home in their pocket torn to shreds by a bullet or explosion; a family devastated by uniformed informers at their front door instead of an expected embrace at the airport.

And for those left behind, those continuing the fight, time has again extended and expired, their stint over; another chance at the changing of the guard.

I Volunteered For This

I volunteered; not just military duty, but for deployment that would fly me halfway around the world. Five years, two wars, no deployments; so I volunteered. The inaugural day of duty brings contemplation on experiences forthcoming outside the wire, feeling exposed and naked sans the safety and protection of a secure facility, what sensations as I head into the proverbial fray.

I volunteered for this!

First request of the day for assistance; the phone rings, the thunderous volume making me jump despite my anticipation. Excitement flows, adrenaline raging as I recall that less than one percent will attain this embarkation, this moment; an enthusiastic rush as I revel in prideful service. In haste to don my gear and snatch up equipment, my contemplation deviates to nervous fervor; I don't want to mess this up, I wish to appear confident and passionate, self-assured and capable in my responsibilities, ready for the mission.

I volunteered for this!

We exit the gate, leaving the security of base behind and begin the short convoy to the unit requesting assistance. Pride and poise depart, altered and replaced with crippling fear of some unidentified attack causing my untimely demise. Distress peaks as I envision the enemy, prepped for violence; anxious in my ability to discern friend from foe, simple man from vicious fighter, civilian from combatant in an unfamiliar city with a people I am unacquainted. Built up anxiety and dread of the unknown are now my companion.

I volunteered for this?

I withdraw from the vehicle, standing inside a four-walled fortress of armor, turrets pointed in every direction, warning and protecting. I stew in unease, awaiting opportunity to complete my duty. Suddenly, a sharp ping off the vehicle next to my head, followed directly by the faintest pop from a building several hundred yards away. I drop, slam my body into the ground as the next round passes overhead, striking the vehicle where I had just been standing. Crawling hurriedly into the vehicle, I slam the door as the turrets roar their deafening response. My breaths come quickly; my eyes search those around me for answers, met with composed discernment of what I will discover is routine. The job completed, we speed back to base, the shelter of tall walls and watch towers.

I volunteered for this?

War; battle; combat; snipers and soldiers and weapons and enemy encounters, all real now. Someone tried to kill me today; my first day, my first mission. I'm hypervigilant, jumpy, tense, on edge, and this will extend into life as I know it. But for now, the phone rings again, the same unit requires aid two hundred meters down the same highway; I am still on duty, there is still a job to do. Adrenaline pumping, lacking my original exhilaration, I gather my equipment and run out the door.

I volunteered for this.

<u>Section 3 – Senses</u>

A warrior's senses, honed to the sensations of battle and warfare, can make the difference between life and death. The memory of a smell or sound from a significant moment can stick with the warrior for the rest of their life. My very first poem in this collection, started on my phone's notepad app, was about the sense of smell. I also penned comparison pieces between silence and noise. I finished several more, completing a majority of the basic human senses, and believe they clearly articulate how they are used during conflict, how they can affect us in post-combat life, and can even provide understanding, empathy, and a connection with our civilian counterparts.

My Pick – "The Smell." This was difficult to pick just one, as I see these particular poems to be some of the most direct, hard-hitting verses that I have wrote. The Smell was my first written poem, and also the first one read by my wife. Her increased understanding of how certain smells could affect me developed into a conversation that I couldn't have had otherwise. The poems enabled the explanations that I couldn't formulate into coherent words, and allowed her an ability to read and ask questions about a topic before starting into a deeper conversation; and that is the reason I kept writing.

The Smell

My nose crinkles; my heart shudders; my brain kicks into gear; and
I know it.
There it is; a smell, *THE* *smell.*

Nobody knows this smell like I do, *my smell*; others have a smell of
their own, this one is mine.
And today, it came for me, like a secret police thump on the door
to deliver me to my internal gulag.

It hits me from nowhere, approaching from this place or that wind,
carried directly to my soul through the piping of my nostrils. And
my soul knows *the smell* all too well; a familiar foe, one of many
antagonists from the past.

As it always does, it perforated my humanity; it tore through walls
built over months and years as though they were nothing but
cardboard mock-ups, falling quickly on a range; it popped that
balloon inside which keeps these secrets and inhaled the contents.
It always does, *the smell.*

It smashes my peace, invades my brain, and destroys all thought
until there is nothing but *the smell*; you see me but I am not there. I
am only *the smell* cloaked in fear and anger and rage as it spills forth
from me and now you, too, are enveloped by *my smell.*

How I wish you could smell it, wish you could comprehend and
recognize *the smell*; how it twists my civility and brings everything
crashing down. And yet, in the same thought, I desire your anosmia
to my smell, to elude the burden it brings; to maintain your own
peace, your own humanity.

The smell; after years it haunts me, and transports me to a place I prefer not revisit. It tears at my nostrils, burns my eyes, and I can taste the torment; my face can feel the hot steam from its mouth like the monster's breath that comes for me at night.

It is *that smell*; of a brother dying in a faraway land, surrounded by blistering heat and violence; of the burnt husk meant to be a mobile protector; of the shattered plated vest and helmet that failed to protect; of blood and gore and burned flesh; of final words, bidding forgiveness and peace, whispering love to pass; of final breaths, stopping and stalling until gone.

I hate, no, I despise…no. I loathe and spurn *the smell*. From the instant it originates to the fury and nightmares that follow, from the burning clot in my throat to the worst memory and harshest exasperation; I detest *my smell*.

But I carry it. One cannot unsoil the memory of a smell with soap and water, or irrigate the recollection with a salty solution and a syringe; so I bring *my smell* as carry-on baggage on life's journey.

Until again, time passes and our noses crinkle; our hearts shudder; and our brains recall ignites again with *THE smell*.

Silence

Without sound, the complete absence of noise, deficient vibrations in the ear drum; silence is a sea of glass unbroken by waves, the dense fog covering a lonesome rural highway, the emptiness of deep space as we journey through the cosmos. It can be achieved in a moment, the constricted headphones just before the music jolts the senses, or showing respect for the departed with bowed head and noiseless tears. Silence is craved, people yearn for the abstinence of utterance, covet the muteness to ease their stress and release their tensions.

But the nature and scope of silence cannot be bound, cannot be restricted and constrained to these descriptions. To those who sign the dotted line, swearing life for brother and country, and now move to defend that promise in a foreign land, silence changes; it deviates from definition, diverges from designation as an abhorrence to be destroyed, a loathsome awakening of the monsters in our minds.

To us, silence lacks clarity; silence raises the warning alarm of unease as we await the coming onslaught, the chaotic anxiety of an unknown direction or form of attack, the confused agitation of unidentified aggression on the battlefield and in your mind. Silence is the discontinuance of a breeze, a disappearance of the usual creatures and beasts lurking, the desertion of crowds, the shuttering of windows; a stillness resounding with the omen that only violence can fulfill.

Silence becomes a persistent ringing, where an increase in silence from cupped hands over covered ears causes resonance intensification; the ringing you hear after a blaring concert parallels the ringing after a piercing gunfight, after the booming explosion, into eternity. Under tension, it becomes a discordant drumbeat, leftover from a resounding chopper ride, stridently thumping with each pump of an irregular heartbeat. Silence becomes a soundless film, the unsynchronized recording of horrifying nightmares performing continuously in the theater of your thoughts.

Silence, both a thunderous rage from a tornadic freight train and a muffled scream caught in the whispers of the wind. The world sleeps while we lay and question what weather the silence will spawn tonight; we long for hurried passage into slumber for the threat of sleeplessness is relentless before the storm. Lying in bed, reposing in the black darkness of night, is no choice, no option as we have learned our bodies must be incessant in task, unceasing in duty to elude the deafening murmurs of silence.

Your peaceful serenity becomes our pained remembrance, where hell opened the gates and the smallest rustle reverberates as Death's raucous stampede to finally collect with scythe in hand. Your noiseless tranquility converges with our unsettling condition, where we overlook our psyche and forget ourselves. You replenish and rejuvenate in the quiet; we suffer in silence.

<u>Silence (Reimagined)</u>

The complete absence of noise,
a sea of unbroken glass and
emptiness of the cosmos.

To you, craving for abstinence of utterance and
coveting a releasing muteness;
peaceful serenity.

But to us, silence deviates definition, diverges designation.

Silence lacks clarity, the chaotic anxiety of unknown attacks;
the disconcerting disappearance of a breeze,
shuttering windows resounding the omen of violence.

Silence resonates persistent ringing, an eternity of echoes;
the discordant drumbeat of irregular heartbeats,
soundless films performing horrifying nightmares in your mind.

Silence spurns thunderous, tornadic rage,
our bodies incessant in task, eluding those deafening murmurs;
the threat of sleeplessness relentless before the storm.

Our pained remembrance, our unsettled condition,
Death's raucous stampede through hell's gates;
we suffer in silence.

The Din

Incessant clamor, loud and prolonged sound, consistent vibrations in the ear drum; the din is a raucous ocean slamming tidal waves onto the shore, the closeness of a rock concert speaker at peak volume, the unruly inferno deep inside the erupting volcano. It can be applied in a moment, effectively garnering attention from even the most boisterous of crowds. The din is repulsed by those who crave peace, resisted for silence and purposely muffled by earplugs or coverings to comfort from strain and pressure.

But the nature and scope of the din cannot be bounded, cannot be restricted and constrained to these descriptions. To those who sign the dotted line, swearing life for brother and country, and now move to defend that promise in a foreign land, the din changes; it deviates from definition, diverges from designation as a disposition to be adored, an affectionate reminder that we have persisted and live to fight another day.

To us, the din brings clarity; the din reduces the uneasy alarm silence can bring, presenting the bearing and form of enemy attack, altering a confused anxiety into resounding understanding, a muddled agitation into a confident advance across the chaos of the battlefield. The din is the shrill screams of a freight train as it thunders down the tracks, a cacophony of angelic voices belting their Godly tune, the uproarious parade as the crowd flees from the resonances of violence we choose to run towards.

The din becomes a harmonious symphony, where an upsurge brings transparency to the nearness of the ensemble of an advancing army; the twig snapping underfoot of the pursued in a soundless forest paralleling the discovered direction of reactive fire to the sniper's position, echoing in the mind of the hunted. Under tension, it expands into a discordant orchestra lacking a conductor, pandemonium with the clanging cymbals arrhythmic to the strident drumbeat. The din becomes a clash of titans, a dreadful scrap of nightmarish giants performing an elaborate composition, drowning out your thoughts.

The din, muddled conversations overpowering our minds and a piercing arrow into the heart of our perceptions. The world listens closely as we tug and wretch at strings within the din, questioning our sanities as we interrogate for the answer; we yearn to smash the mass of discordant sounds if only to hear ourselves think. Always learning, permanently entrenched in erudition, is our only option as we must gain the intellect and wisdom it takes to overcome the din, to dismiss the earsplitting background that pushes against the door of our minds.

Your tumultuous commotion becomes our saving grace, where heaven opens the gates and the trumpet's fanfare of a repeated incoming…incoming…incoming remigrates Death and his scythe back to the fiery pits of hell. Your turbulent static converges with our preferred dissonance, as the loquacious murmur wakes us from the haze, evoking our psyche from the brink after a deafening explosion. You fatigue and regress from the noise; we are reminded of our survival in the din.

<u>The Eyes</u>

The eyes; the visual organs that conceal inner agony and yet ceaselessly speak the truth, the anatomical processors of light that afford the open doors to our humanity. The eyes are the brain's instrument to perceive the world, bringing clarity to light and understanding to darkness, discerning the dazzling detail and beholding the beautiful brushstrokes of land and sky. Beyond vision, the eyes communicate, declare with booming echoes and whisper in muted silence, their variation in direction exposing the very nature of our thoughts. The eyes are the influential authority of memories, intermingling with supplementary senses to weave a thorough reminiscence that plays as a motion picture in our mind.

The eyes; our observable capacity when taking aim down our sights, our ultimate power over dulled sanities in the midst of battle. The eyes are our witness to billowing smoke after a concussive explosion; our viewing pane to the downtown market sprayed red and pink with the blood of local shoppers; our regard to the now-parentless child staring back through our windows, the eyes betraying sadness and disgust; the ascertaining pupil seeing empty streets and shuttered windows predicting another imminent attack. At war, our eyes distinguish friend and foe, brother and enemy; they spy the pockmarked vehicle and chipped glass showing a foe's futile attack; they detect the friendly chopper shot down in a field, the ensuing inferno taking all lives aboard; they notice the captured enemy pleading for their freedom and life, and the brother's slumped shoulders, weary after a long-fought battle.

At the height of conflict, the eyes learn diverse and unwelcome sights; the lone, shadowy hole marking the entrance of the sniper's bullet; the pained expression of the wounded soldier, absent his leg from the knee down; the room occupied by lifeless enemy fighters after the grenade seals their fate; the bowed heads of prayerful remembrance opposite the stage adorned with a dozen battlefield crosses.

The eyes; their faded colors surrounded by collective creases tell stories no words can articulate, express haunted memories and painful reminiscences best forgotten. They gaze into a bottomless space of nothingness, glimpse unknowingly at the indifferent dot on the horizon, spotting figments of friends long since gone, catching slips into former combat realities, and anticipating the nightmares that always follow. In the twilight, the eyes watch through thousand yard stares atrocities and horrors beyond the imagination of television screens or movie directors; only those who have discovered the degeneration of mortality can truly see through our eyes.

<u>The Weight</u>

I carry the weight, so you don't have to.

I carry this weight in my hands, the laden palms holding a ten pound death dealer and personal protector, the loaded rifle equal the mass of the sniper's weapon that landed the dying gunner in my lap, his last breaths taken in my arms. I carry this weight on my chest, the overloaded pectorals drained by the thirty pound bulletproof guardian, the thick body armor hampered with equipment equal the heft of the suicide vest that triggered and massacred dozens in that downtown market.

I carry the weight, so you don't have to.

I carry this weight on my back, the muscle weighed down by my fifty pound pack for a multi-day mission, the heavy gear equal the bulk of the fiery projectile that exploded beneath the vehicle, killing the first friend I witnessed perish in combat. I carry this weight on my shoulders and neck, the totality of the nearly hundred pound strain adding to gravity's downward pull, my entire encumbrance equal my screaming brother's hemorrhaging form thrown over my shoulders as we cross the Devil's passage of flying lead, bleeding bodies, and extreme strife.

I carry the weight, so you don't have to.

I carry this weight despite the restriction to my freedom of movement, just as it can restrict my cerebral sovereignty from the images that haunt my dreams. I carry this weight despite the limitations to my joint mobility, just as the traumatic tension and pressure add debilitating strain on my physical form. I carry this weight despite the reduction to my visibility, just as my apprehension reduces my aptitude to see situations appropriately. I carry this weight despite the delays to my response time, just as my thoughts and my emotions are delayed in their healing. I carry this weight despite the fatigue, despite the exhaustion, just as the draining and sapping stress causes the bone-deep weariness in my soul.

I carry this weight as my responsibility of burden, my obligation to those who didn't come home, my compulsion to the generations of warriors, a sign of my commitment and duty as one who has seen the slaughter of civilization, the carnage of humanity, and stared Death in his shadowed face but was allowed to live.

I carry the weight, all day, every night, and will through the twilight of my life, so you don't have to.

<u>Section 4 – Aftermath</u>

At no time in history have we had more information on and more in-depth study into the post-combat mind of warriors. Some of these verses are highly personal, and relate to experiences I still have to this day from my combat service. Other verses are a general understanding of the outcomes and repercussions of combat from fellow veterans as I have heard or read their stories over the years. As a reminder, this section speaks directly to the instances and effects of combat PTSD and could be inferred to other forms of PTSD as well, so understand that the writing is meant to be dramatic, intense, and may cause high levels of emotion and recalls.

My Pick – "The First Week of December." Most of these aftermath poems are personal accounts, but none more personal than the first week of December. This is the time of year that is most difficult for me in my constant struggle with the thoughts, emotions, and memories of combat. In just a short couple of days, my unit took some hard hits and earned a dreadful designation as the highest casualty rate seen in an Air Force unit in combat since the Vietnam era. Add in that December has always been a month of struggle through the holidays from personal tragedies and family deaths, and you can better understand the volatile condition of my mind during this week.

<u>The First Week of December</u>

As life passes, as days and months go by faster and faster like a never-ending freight train bearing down the tracks of time, a stretch of the year arises that disturbs, that troubles the veteran, that teases their mind perennially until they are standing at the threshold of anguish and the door of those memories opens.

My time has come. It has come to pass before, this haunting period, ripping and tearing the scars from my recollection until crimson red streaks blind my inner vision.

And as always, this time is a noiseless mendicant, beseeching the glorious silence between turkey and tinsel, between stuffed sustenance and early-morning elation, between the Thanksgiving feast and the Christmas pine. My time, the first week of December.

This time is a screen, blocking the forgone phase of celebrations, family, and friends. My recall is devastated, the screen tattered only by images of battlefield crosses, two side-by-side or a platform of five, all standing taller than the soldiers kneeling before them. My unwavering focus on the upended rifle, capped by a helmet, slung with dog tags, surrounded with sentiments from still-standing brothers, and abutted by the combat boots nobody can fill.

This time is the opening of hunting season, discharging its barrel in the bullseye of my conscience, assassinating my inner armistice between the past and the present with a volley of emotions, each center mass strike transporting me back to my brothers' memorial; each potshot round a reminder of my unit's highest casualty count.

This time is an ulcer, an acidic exhale in my throat that breathes my nightmare into existence; the sour flavor of the foulest of snapshots my memory has taken through absent Humvee armor, depicting the charred interior plastered with an insidious pink paste; a rancorous palate as I transfix on the serenely sleeping gunner with the filthy face, and the bitter flavor of swallowing bile as my gaze drops for my foremost look inside the gunner's lower body having been evenly halved; each acrimonious grasp for oxygen a reminder of a congested, standing-room theater, choked with inner strife and tears as we faced the inexplicable bereavements presented on the stage.

My time has passed. I stretch forward, hopeful the subsequent holiday can clot and stem the crimson flow of my reminiscence; I reach out my arms to dismantle the screen, to strip the weapon, to medicate the open sores of my mind until I return to the threshold next year, in the first week of December.

<u>Avoidance</u>

My purposeful actions remove the undesirable, avoid the situational, circumvent the conversational until I am safe, until escape eliminates, until evasion eradicates and I withdraw into myself. I dive and duck one-sided dodgeball attacks, diverting from uncomfortable and deflecting dread and anxiety with maladaptive coping no shrink can break through. This behavior protects me, from thinking those thoughts, from feeling those feelings and sanctions the sidestep, skirting around the stressors and damage of my unexposed trauma.

I elude discussions, eschew topics that expose wounds that never healed, that bares an injured soul. Tit-for-tat, the back-and-forth match where they serve their questions and I swing to change subjects, they volley their dialogue and I spike my lacking will with bypassing finality.

My cornered conscious counts exits, purposely parks facing the ingress and nearest the exodus to shake the onslaught, avert the ambush on my weary humanity that carries this burden. My preventive tactics defend my barricade from television dramatics and movie theatrics, preserve my blockade constructed of tortured outlooks and pained remembrance from these scenes that rehash an epoch best forgotten.

I will not tolerate, will not submit and abide to the possibility of reexperience, the prospect of reliving the haunting of my dreams; avoidance is my acquaintance, my associate who preserves my peace.

The Recurring Nightmare

I'm up. Sweat pouring like a spring rain and soaking the bedsheets, shaking uncontrollably like I was left naked in the freezing arctic; but at least I'm awake, and not there. I notice my heart pounding in my chest and head, uncontrolled and palpitating; I recognize my breath, rapid like I just crossed the marathon's finish line; my mind is panicked, anxiety is peaked, apprehension and unease breaking my own internal records; my body is tight, locked and loaded to spring into action yet exceedingly sore, aching from the unceasing readiness of my red alert status.

This is my recurrent shell shock, my persistent post-traumatic stress, my frequent and unwelcome visitor; often the same situation, the identical location, unchanged circumstances of feeling and seeing the frailty of life snuffed by the severity of war. Other sufferers trudge through their own intrusive reminders and flashbacks, each specific to the individual experience of severe trauma to body or sight or mind.

This is my recurring nightmare.

The call comes in at night, a pitch black evening beneath a cloud-covered moon. The temperature is cold, the chilly wind biting at your exposed skin despite the surrounding desert landscape. We hastily don our combat accessories, gather our gear, as our duty is to be through the door and outside the wire as quickly as possible; the victim convoy and its surviving personnel are waiting on us. We gather with our dedicated security team, a hurried brief on the route and prayer from the chaplain for mission success and personal safety, a rushed loading of up-armored trucks and check of the comms, a speedy drive through the gate and the clacking of rounds being chambered; and into the fray I go again.

Nearly an hour north, a patrolling unit struck by a large explosive device; three killed in action, two critically wounded, already being rushed to doc; this call nothing out of the norm for that time in East Baghdad. We mulled this information as we rushed to the scene, ever-watchful to the roadsides for the bomb meant for us, continually alert to the surrounding flashes of scenery as we drive on. We arrive, a juncture of multi-lane highways connecting at a slightly uphill intersection, a brightly lit sector empty of vehicles due to the curfew but dangerously luminous for night operations, a four-point cordon of Humvees and tanks providing an armed barrier to the outside world. We park within the blockade in our own four-tiered protective defense, allowing the explosive experts a shielded zone to remove their robot to verify safety from additional explosive threats. There's none; I'm up.

I exit the vehicle, grabbing my weapon and gear. Perhaps due to the cold, perhaps to the smell, perhaps to the danger of a brightly lit scene, only one explosive expert teammate and I have withdrawn from the warmth of the Humvee interior. His hands are on his weapon, eyes on streets and alleys and rooftops while my hands carry the camera, jot notes and distances, eyes on the scene. The scene is still fresh; the smell of the burnt husk of an up-armored vehicle blends with scorched human skin and the ever-constant aroma of garbage.

Quickly, I snap picture after picture, four cardinal directions to later provide a rough sketch of location, an overview of the broken vehicle from the driver's side to provide an accurate record of the original scene, close-ups of the blast crater and enormous opening the bomb left in the rear driver's side door, along with measurements for size and shape. The smell is stronger; I can see the blood mixed with gas and oil covering the ground and the bottom of my boots; the windshield and windows are covered in crimson and pink splatter and chunks; a scene all too familiar, I lower my head and walk around the charred vehicle for the final piece of the investigation.

And it happens; what I consider the principal motive for the recurrence of this scene. The passenger door is open, the other door blown off completely, and my view is the full extent of brutal destruction inflicted within. I snap only one picture, my only requirement, but I cannot tear my eyes away. Human pieces and parts strewn throughout the vehicle; gory spray and clumps of internal tissue dispersed across every interior surface; pools of dark blood on seats, floorboards, and surrounding ground; even this considered somewhat common in those days. But the difference is the gunner; cut directly in half by the projectile, his upper half rests vertically atop a horizontal pair of hips and legs. I can gaze at his soot-covered face and inside his lower torso simultaneously; his hands are clenched as though still holding his heavy gun atop the vehicle; his face shows a wounded grimace, frozen in a pained wince; his eyes are closed. Troubled, I turn away, but as I do gunfire erupts from a distant rooftop and bullets kick up concrete and clang into metal. Security elements return fire immediately, the deafening din drowning out my teammate's entreaties to move faster. The scene is no longer safe; I need to get back to the truck.

Suddenly the gunner's eyes open; blue, familiar eyes looking through long eyelashes from a thin face with a long nose. It's me. Through an open door, I watch a figure turn and run as the crackle of gunfire erupts, both distant and near. I try to call out; silence. I try to move; I can't. I can only see the inhuman devastation surrounding me as I recognize that my friends, my brothers are gone.

And then I'm up; sweaty, panicked, uneasy with ragged breath; but at least I am awake, and not there.

<u>The Night I Should've Quit Drinking</u>

I was back; back to heat, back to putrid hotness that envelopes like an insincere hug from a malevolent devil; back to sand, back to grit and gravel that blows in the wind, piercing your eyes and parching your mouth; back to sounds, back to screeching tires, explosive concussions that disable your ears, an overhead commencement of the appeal to Allah that was our daily acquaintance.

I was here; here at the party, listening to music so loud it restricted conversation unless you screamed your words; playing the game, beer pong and darts and bags and washers, anything to keep the revelry entertaining; slamming my drinks, choking back the shitty beer from the game while sipping whiskey after whiskey to dehydrate my feelings, to fiery shot after shot that burned as they attempted to drown my emotions; here with friends and acquaintances, rare people you care for divided with those you just met.

Then again, I was back; back to the cut scene, post blast; back to disorientation surged by pain, confusion, and fear; back to self-investigation, back to looking for red, smelling for iron, and trying to identify agony through foggy senses; back to sluggish clarity, the abysmal understanding of occurrence; back to my brothers, back to inquiring, probing, shouting to collect the four voices expected.

I stayed back; back to a cracked windshield, back to a view of a smoking behemoth lying sideways in the street; back to gunfire, back to an eruption of lethal lead manifested from several directions yet aimed down the throat of the behemoth; back to open doors, the behemoth's jaws producing bloody and burnt shadows, and on my left as my feet slammed the asphalt the same time as my ribs to evade the incoming fire; back to basic, back to where I first learned the lowest crawl that transported me near the behemoth, to my brother's aid.

With no thought, I was thrown here; here in lifting arms, here with those rare friends who raised me from the apartment complex parking lot pavement; here with my confusion, the staggering, stammering, stabilizing, starting, stopping, staring, until finally succumbing to the rupture in my belly; here at the party, songs all but faded, competitions ceased, friends and acquaintances staring rifts through my misunderstanding; here with my disgrace, my shame and scandal in a chair by the door, awaiting my night's fate.

And I cannot fathom how, I was back; back in a crossfire, trapped in a tornado of shrapnel, theirs and ours, ours and theirs, flying directly above me.

And I cannot say why, I was here; here in my own crossfire, trapped in an argument of staying or leaving, of a night in a friend's musty guest lodging or the comfort of my own kingdom.

And again, I was back; back in and out of the behemoth, back to barking for doc and searching out the next vacant seat to stuff another bloody and burnt shadow into, eavesdropping to catch if doc thought this faceless shadow would survive.

And again, I was barely here; here in the real world, barking for my accompaniment to join in the taxi that just arrived, being stuffed into the weave-covered back seat, eavesdropping to hear that I would get home safe.

Back; back to convoying quickly through the empty night streets toward our temporary home, speeding past light post after light post, always scrutinizing the curbs for the evil that triggered this chaos.

Here; riding through the city toward my neighborhood, staring at street light after street light as they passed, scrutinizing curbs that held only litter and used cigarettes.

I was endlessly back; back to darkness, the depth of the deepest ocean; back to black, holding onto me with the grip of a cancerous mole on your skin; back to nothing, a forgotten void where insidious trips of bygone days disappeared and going back ceased to exist.

Scars

A mark soaked into skin from a wound or burn not wholly healed or a blemished epidermal replacement post-injury, a scar is visualized as the biological repair process, a finishing touch at the mechanic's shop of your human form. This marred discoloration the consequence of harm, a natural and predictable stain of the body's bruised rind. This tegumental doppelganger is by composition dissimilar, divergent from original tissue and lacks the standard elasticity to adapt to its environment. With little exception, these impairments and contusions, lacerations and disturbances result in some degree of imperfection, some aggregate of distortion that fashions a new normal.

Visually, one can see the hypertrophic rosy bump rising from the warped surface of the soldier's face, grazed by Death's scythe and the sniper's rifle, or the scalp left wanting for hair and stained abrasions observed on the pained scarfskin of the burned warrior. Clearly grasped is the absent appendage with folded and tucked sleeve or trouser leg, silently accepting its idleness dearth its master. Exceptionally evident is the wheelchair-bound veteran, returning from their bout with demise sporting strong upper limbs and wheels that fill the deformed void pilfered by the concussive explosion. These deep scars, these twisted remnants of human flesh and bone wrench on surrounding healthy tissue, disfiguring even that which was uninjured and torturing its sovereign with apparitional sensations of its existence.

Hidden from view but still discernable on the mortal surface, the soldier veils minor scars, seeking humility of strength from shrapnel in their leg, craving recognition of persistent endurance vice attributed weakness from the bullet that smashed

58

their shoulder. Yearning for covertness in their malady drives the damage into seclusion, the casualty camouflaged by outward appearance despite anatomical pain in every stride, structural discomfort in every swing. Even further designated are surface scars, cosmetic cicatrix unencumbered in form or function, exposed only as irrefutable evidence of the veteran's distressing account.

But beyond epithelial layers of the corporeal form, within the bark shell of the tree of life, the scar's trademark becomes invisibility, hidden within heartwood at the center tree ring, obscured in darkness at the depths of the soul. Imperceptible behind pained eyes, the soldier's invisible scar hints a false humility, eclipsing expectations of strength and persistence with permanent alterations of the mind. The battering of intellect, a mauling of one's humanity, secretly defaces the casualty's brain; an unexposed trauma, a concealed flaw until actions and confrontations scream custodial release, disfiguring even the sturdiest of relationships, torturing its sovereign with cloaked existence, and exposing a veteran's distress disguised in rage and vagaries.

Body or mind, physical and metaphysical, just because you heal does not mean there isn't a scar.

<u>Scars (Reimagined)</u>

A biological repair process, the scar soaks into skin,
a blemishing epidermal replacement;
the discolored consequence of harm;
the human form's stained rind.

Impairments drive imperfection, aggregate distortion for a new
normal.

Visually, Death's grazing scythe warps the surface,
absent appendages silently accept idleness,
strong arms and wheels fill a deformed void.
Twisted remnants torture their sovereign with apparitional
sensations of existence.

Superficial, soldiers veil minor maladies,
driving shrapnel damage into seclusion,
camouflaging the appearance of casualty.
Anatomical pain, structural discomfort yearning for covertness in
their endurance.

Invisible, hidden within heartwood and obscured in darkness,
imperceptible behind pained eyes, the unexposed trauma.
Battering intellect, mauling humanity,
a cloaked existence exposed, disguised as rage and vagaries.
Indiscernible, permanent alterations of the mind;
the casualty's concealed scar.

<u>The Stigma</u>

My internal scars define me. I return from war, return from corporeal battle with death and destruction and explosions and firefights and blood and loss and survival and fear, and they express that I am different, changed, altered in my demeanor and mentality, questioning things that I saw or did. I flush red, instantly consumed with rage and anger at their judgment, what would you expect to happen?! They convey shock and surprise, voice concern for my outlash, unease of my outburst, alarm at my eruption, and utter the words I loathe: seek help.

These people, these shadows of leadership and friendship surrounding me, misunderstand the trauma from combat. Clueless for how to deal with post-traumatic stress, baffled for how to handle stressful memories or scarring experiences or damaging thoughts and recollections, bewildered at my inability to just turn it off, my incapacitation from conflict and confrontation; just one answer, the single retort that shows my internal scars define me.

The weight of crushing stigmas anchors my thoughts, pushes my shoulders down in a hunched stance, depresses my disposition and deforms my temperament until the shell begins to crack. My warrior identity is at once humiliated and ashamed, my mentality wounded and demeaned to be defined by my weakness, forced to pursue unwarranted and unwanted support. My duty suffers, the job must be completed at all costs, tough it out, make it work, figure that shit out; my craving to follow that which I have been taught devastated by my mortification. Others' struggles are worse than mine and deserve treatment first, my career may suffer from this mandatory disgrace, my justifications fail to convince deaf ears; I'm fine, I am fine with my internal scars defining me.

But I went. Despite everything, despite fear and loathing and struggle and shame and humiliation and discomfort and disgrace and embarrassment, I went. And I encounter zero understanding with indifferent empathy; a caring tone dissonant to resonation or relation with the melee of my thoughts and memories; a therapist who has never deployed, is physically unable to fight, whose initial response is to throw prescriptions at my post-traumatic problems, medication at malevolence in my mind; whose idea of effective communication is the gentlest of tenors to compete against fury and wrath building from my stomach to my throat about to spew forth; I walk out, knowing what those reports will say…my internal scars define me.

I'm not deployed, but my mind continues the war, alone in my head wrestling against thoughts and emotions and anxiety and feelings and reminders and stress and pressure and nightmares; torture in isolation and sorrow in silence. Injuries require treatment but invisible to the naked eye, I easily conceal damage, obscure the wound so it is simply overlooked; on the inside, unseen, unheard, where my internal scars can define me.

The Screams I Hear

The screams arrive periodically, returning from the depths of memory from time to time as aggrieved remembrance, an unsettling commemoration to a night best forgotten. Despite a craving for elapsed years to suppress visions and dull the volume, haunting and piercing, the screams wake me from slumber; not the soft wailing or pitched bawling of an infant that rouse the resting mother, rather the earsplitting, unforgettable shrieks of the wounded soldier from the battlefield.

This boy, no older than 19, remains screeching in my sleeping reminiscence. His boyish face pinched tight in agony, his strong hand intensely clasping mine in pained anguish, his torso and lower extremities firmly strapped to the stretcher and draped with a thin, blood-soaked blanket to avoid flailing and the spectacle of his missing limb; these images and sensations stagnate in my ruminating nightmare.

One hand in his, the other holding the stretcher, we leap from the truck and rush him to the waiting medical chopper. Every clumsy trip or hard footfall of any of the foursome of bearers brings blood-curdling yells of suffering. Once at the door, the medic has to tear his grip from my hand to get him emplaced, bumping him against partitions and floor that brings forth roars of distraught contention. As the door closes, I hear over swirling wind his final distressed screams and the chopper lifts away.

I'm awake; although my room is silent and tranquil, lingering cries continue to ring in my ears like a shrill whistle won from the fair in my youth. I picture his tense expression and feel his handhold slip away as my mind draws a portrait of the rising helicopter. I yearn for rest, sleep without nightmares, slumber without these manifestations attacking my mind and soul; but I know, ultimately, my thoughts will again recall the screams.

More Thoughts

This final section contains supplemental poems with varied topics. Most of them relate to my military service or the profession of arms in general, and a couple were written simply because of how I felt that day or the idea had spurned off of another verse I was writing at the time.

My often daily pursuit for the bottom of a bottle is like a poacher with no tag, hunting all that he deems desirable. The bottle's label makes no difference, the matter of brand only important as a factor of quantity I can purchase. Type and flavor vary, as taste belies the underlying swift success of the content's effects. The bottle's shade, clear or colored white or red or yellow or green or brown, is forgotten so long as the change from opaque to transparent as liquid disappears conveys to me to open another.

These contents deliver solace to my weary soul, to the battle-hardened veteran aching for peace, to the fatigued soldier yearning to forget. I covet the comfort from pain in the muddled thoughts, relief from discomfort in the jumbled moods given only upon the pinnacle of the upturned bottle. My days are long, infatuated with the start of a new flask, pining for the substance that makes consciousness and life habitable. I survive to summit the peak over and again with an inverted and emptied bottle in my grasp.

Yet this illegitimate apex, this spurious zenith spawns an unforeseen trough of prolonged nights that stretch into perpetuity. The withering memories enhance, gain traction in my brain; they pass on the inside, cutting me off as I crash into the wall of my recollections. Robust and strong, retentions become reality as I flashback to hell; and as quickly as I coveted that comfort, my collision compels me back to the place I aimed to forget. I'm stuck, popping another cork as the residue left from the previous bottle becomes the damaged trust of my closest friends; the last drops of whiskey the final straw for loved ones reaching out; the broken fragments as the bottle smashes into the wall, a lost career, another life taken by my attempts to outrun my demons in a car, my own meeting with Death's scythe as I drink into oblivion.

I hate and abhor what I discover at the bottom of a bottle; yet here I am, decanter in fist, seeking that reprieve from agony in the disarray provided by the bottle.

<u>Time I</u>

One second, the infinitesimal blink of an eye, the low-toned solitary click of the ever-rotating hand on a timepiece, the soundless descent of a single grain of sand in Father Time's hourglass. To you, this is the fleeting glimpse from the attractive soul at the end of the bar or the quick, delightful reaction of a dozen smiling muscles in a baby's expression. To us, a momentary indication from the passing wind that a bullet missed or the blinding flash of immense pressure as roadside garbage detonates beside us.

One minute, a collection of sixty specks of time, a miniscule turn of the largest hand on a wristwatch, a standard for the New York lifecycle and the indication of health and life as the requisite record of heartbeats in your chest. To you, this is the sunrise routine of straightening sheets, comforters, and pillows or the forced delay as you impatiently wait at a red traffic signal. To us, a temporary phase between bomb ignition and intellect sufficiently clear to check for a crimson stain or hurrying a screaming brother, bound in tourniquets and strapped to a stretcher, to the circling armored knight that can assist in his escape.

One hour, three score of sluggish, spherical movements around the wall clock, a lone mile of a diurnal marathon, the upper glass bulb emptied as the King of Titans reluctantly resumes the sands of time with the turn of his wrist. To you, this is the loathsome conclusion to midday mealtimes as you trudge back to the grind or the summation of family entertainment viewing their program on evening television. To us, the transitory passage from green to red to black ammunition in a deadly firefight or a white-knuckled drive lacking armor across a landscape of lethal projectiles devised to destroy and assassinate.

One day, the shadows resurrected across the sun dial as sunrise appears and dark withdraws, the full rotation of the earth to attest that the moon survived the exclusion of our presence, an awakening cockcrow at dawn to the wolves howling their nightly lullaby. To you, this is nine-to-five employment bracketed by familial tasks and personal errands or the mark of your sunset routine with the calendar's subsequent X. To us, a caffeine-laden Groundhog Day where the war is relentless, repeating one midnight to the next or the communication blackout where outside correspondence ceases until those escorting our fallen brother home can commence military bereavement with the toughest knock on a front door.

One week, a consecutive sevensome of dawns and dusks, a stretch of 40-hour drudgery succeeded by a spell of respite, a cantankerous initiation to the grind through the camel's fatty backbone to the stint where God rested from his creation. To you, this is the abhorrent delay between a cliffhanger episode and a spectacular sitcom conclusion or a freshly trimmed lawn and backyard barbeque with friends celebrating the breather from school and labor. To us, a perpetual, entropic series of workdays extending into an unceasing eternity where combat never sleeps or the expected duration of resupply convoy operations on the Highway of Death, still littered with decades-old husks of scorched military equipment that could once again return to glory as vehicle-born explosions.

One month, the intervals fashioned to synchronize the seasons, the cyclic tetrad of toiling routine, the predictable lunar phases waxing from a dim crescent slice to an illuminated corpulent orb. To you, this is an obligation of recompense for a running tap and electrical power or Mother Nature's feminine visitation providing her painful souvenir. To us, another notched tally mark conveying the ever-proximate culmination of our sentence or an oft-forgotten circadian variation in the unyielding battle encircling the defenses of our outposts and minds.

One year, a dozen variations of the hanging kitchen calendar, a time-reckoned tradition of reclaiming contrived levies, the protracted quartet of winters that turn into spring and summers that turn into fall. To you, this is the annual celebration on the anniversary of birth or the proclaimed resolution of improvement or sacrifice to author the fresh chapter. To us, a changing of the guard as we grudgingly summon fresher troops to answer the coming void or an epoch's end that ultimately leaves us with weary bodies and shattered minds.

<u>Time II</u>

A second, infinitesimally tiny compared to a month; a minute, hundreds of thousands times smaller than a year; an hour, miniscule equated to a century. Yet as time passes, as fresh warriors relieve soldiers redeploying home, as spring blossoms into the warmth of summer and autumn descends into frigid winter, we discover that Father Time deceives us. He fabricates the diminutive minutes when millennia pass as we await a doctor's cancer prognosis; he falsifies the hour with a horizontal turn of the hourglass so we sense eternity in a brief firefight. Time is assumed, not understood, and is implicit in this betrayal.

Time is entropic, chaotic and disorderly, often a tasteless game the King of Titans manipulates at will. A new dawn to the setting sun where nothing transpires, paralleling the sloth's movements, but the following daybreak to midnight hour fits four seasons' worth of tasks and activities. Professor after professor's droning lecture drags the day uphill through muddy hours, yet the manic downhill deterioration at the Battle of Mogadishu aged the surviving soldier years in a single October day.

Time is a jumbled space, a confused expanse between two outstretched galaxies thrust within a thimble. The succeeding year appears vastly distant to the encaged teenager anticipating a license to drive or the spouse awaiting the soldier's homecoming from deployment. But for the rotating soldier, a year home with family looks infinitely minute as they depart yet again for conflict. A solitary second too late swerving from the bomb's explosion seems a universe apart from the preceding second's security, yet the identical second and slight swivel of the head can decide life over death as the sniper's bullet glances off a helmet.

Time is an unruly race, a muddled competition with no tangible winner as all eventually lose the lawless battle, defeated by the perpetually advancing movement of the clock. The briefest of seconds as the hare sprints from gunshot to finish line diverges from the laggard minutes of waiting on hold when the topic is of the utmost importance. The lengthiest of hours as the tortoise crawls each mile of a marathon contrasts the swiftness of multiple decades of service as the veteran retires with a longing glance at past endeavors.

As years grow into decades and decades into lifetimes, as hours and days stretch into infinity yet months and years rapidly vanish, as the timeworn veteran salutes the green recruit, time is both an ageless, God-given inheritance and a wanton, biased squandering to be slayed by Death's scythe. Eras and millennia will continue to pass, battles and wars will continue to rage, as old Father Time deceives us once again.

<u>My Plea</u>

Before I go, spend time with me in positive experiences, constructive conversations, cherished memories that will help us all get through the months ahead. Talk to me, tell me your fears, your emotions without hinting your disgust for the one thing I have volunteered my life to do, without overstating illogical entreaty to stay or run away; trust that my fears, my emotions run rampant as well and my preference is always you. Service to our country comes with sacrifice; this is the life I chose, and you chose me. Stay close, stay nearby, stay present, even as my commitment to duty drives longer hours; remember that I am training to survive. This is my plea.

While gone, don't hasten to think the worst when I am quiet; I may not be allowed to call, and the day's experiences may be the heaviest of burdens on my brain. When I do call, let me listen to your voices, hear your stories, eavesdrop on the events of your day and week; I miss the sounds of home and don't want my voice, my troubles to drown them out. Be a mainstay of strength in your toughest hours; I will wish to resolve the problems and find your solutions, distressing over your difficulties when my concentration is required for duty, for survival. I know, I understand, I comprehend and appreciate the weight you carry every day I am gone; but one stray thought can mean life or death for my brothers and me. This is my plea.

When I return, don't take my silence personally; don't rankle at my irrational irritation or absurd annoyance as I wrestle with the emotions of my return; don't fester in my muteness as I contemplate my survival. As much as I needed you as my rock while deployed, I require your dedicated devotion, your stalwart strength, your persistent patience to linger through this processing stage, to hang on while I gather those parts of my mind and soul lost or shoved aside, ensuring my unfaltering focus on getting home. This is my plea.

As the years pass, as the dust from my gear settles to the bottom of the deployment bag heaved into the basement corner, there will be times, instances, moments, phases where your abilities as a strong pillar must stand tall again. I will pine to suffer in silence; don't let me. I will crave personal space; be there when I'm ready. I will ache to resign, wish to quit, want for abandon; tenderly push me, as my hidden desire will always be to return to you whole, unabridged and complete. This is my final plea.

<u>Our Why</u>

Our collective souls fought humanity's battles from east to west, from Great Wars of the past to remote operations at home and abroad; we continue these battles from here to eternity. We live the exceptional life, the uncommon one percent who serve for liberty of the ninety-nine, with precious few fighting at the weary battlefront. Despite our communal service, *why* we serve is often more detached, separate and disconnected from our brethren's response to the identical question; *why?*

We serve for honor, for the esteem and respect afforded those adhering to stringent standards of conduct and glorified through notable achievements and sacrifice;

We serve for challenge, answering the plea, responding to the call, partaking in duty that matures us quickly, strengthens us physically, and prepares us mentally;

We serve for family, for generations of warriors or a fresh inheritance, for the old we leave behind as we march into battle and the new by our side as we face the enemy;

We serve for self, for the university bill we cannot afford on our own, a fresh start, for the pay and benefits and entitlements we could not find on the outside;

We serve for knowledge, for the top-notch training and skills we earn, for worldly understanding as we study and travel through God's creation;

We serve for peace, enforcing law and order to deter conflict, applying structure to disorderly imbalance, for the tranquil freedom from a life well-spent;

We serve for trust, the constructed reliability of brothers and sisters in arms, for the credit allotted by our true customers, the people;

We serve for country, the star-spangled nation and land of our immigrant legacy, for the protection of the distinctive red, white, and blue waving gloriously overhead;

We serve for mission, our purpose for existence, a disciplined and selfless intent, for the summation of goals and objectives that shape the future;

We serve for love, an intense affection for humankind, an internal pride and self-esteem, for the pleasure of infatuation with the land, sea, sky, or beyond;

We serve for freedom, earning the absence of subjection or imprisonment, our gift to the world, for God-given rights without undue restraint;

We serve for camaraderie, fighting alongside the man on our left and the woman on our right, for the mutual bonds of pained solidarity and shared experience;

Why do we serve? We serve for this, and so much more…

<u>To The 22</u>

You don't know me.
But today, I heard your story.
I wish you were still here.

You were the first story I was told, the first to be so bold,
To think this was the way to depart from where you stood.
Basic did not appear so tough, but for you it seemed so rough,
And before your brothers could help, you were gone for good.

Then came the first duty station, as we fought to serve the nation,
You broke the marriage rule and became unstable.
The girl ended up with child, a missing man and gun, beguiled,
And through the barrel, we saw an empty chair at the briefing table.

You don't know me.
But today, I heard your story.
I wish you were still here.

We attended the prestigious schools, several years of hard knocks and
rules,
But we never considered it so harsh it would cause us to break.
You hooked that cord around the rafter, breaking into an unknown
hereafter,
And your family left only with the action you decided to take.

Once again we go into the fray, off to a war, come what may,
Into a desert, or jungle, or trench bursting with strife.
You saw brothers die every day, bleeding out, passing away,
And after those nightmares, we found the bottle that ended your life.

You don't know me.
But today, I heard your story.
I wish you were still here.

You left the service before me, ten years paid was your fee,
Received your honorable discharge and moved on, looking for more.
But your anxiety came back to haunt you, depression the straw that
you drew,
And in the darkness you drained your wrists on the bathroom floor.

You don't know me.
But today, I heard your story.
I wish you were still here.

Twenty years of service to country, your citizen persona a little rusty,
You were just months from a new life on the outside.
Your worries mounted higher and higher, dragging you down in the
muck and mire,
And you swerved that bike into the traffic with which you'd collide.

You don't know me.
But today, we heard your story.
We wish you were still here.

Your body has been broken and bent, now the VA is where you are
sent,
Seeking help and amends for your mental and physical pain.
You waited forever, they refused to assist, so down the stairs you
went, not missed,
And those meant to support you, found you lifeless outside in the
rain.

You don't know me.
But today, the nation heard your story.
We wish you were still here.

My best friend for over 10 years, we had a connection, and jokes, and tears,
I wait for every call to catch up, knowing my spirit will climb.
But this late call was a different sort, you had thoughts to cut your life short,
But you chose to chat instead, and thank God, I answered in time.

You know me.
And today, I remember your story.
I'm happy you are still here.

A co-worker from just down the hall, we barely knew each other at all,
Our talks of life and combat were spoken mostly in passing.
Some days and dreams hit hard, knowing your brain is injured and marred,
But you reached out, we found the right comfort, now your dream's less harassing.

You know me.
And today, I remember your story.
I'm happy you are still here.